A LITTLE HAIKU

Miranda Leigh

DEDICATIONS HAIKU:

My shady sister
May you always find silver
Linings, always light

To my creators
Where would I be without you
Grateful for your love

My one and only
My other half, my soulmate
Feel my words, my love

Beautiful Daughter
Of mine, how lucky am I
To be your mother

No. 1

Stillness swarms, surrounds
Buzz with wanderlust within
Desire to break free

No. 2

In the morning light
Tangled sheets, love uncovered
Warm breath, waking skin

No. 3

Grateful for each sip
I drink from the glass, half full
Thirsty yet, for more

MIRANDA LEIGH

No. 4

Bare bones broken down
By the side of the road, lost
Waiting for something

No. 5

Painting all the shades
Self reflections left behind
Floating in the sea

MIRANDA LEIGH

No. 6

Sometimes love prevails
Exceeds all expectations
Sometimes love prevails

No. 7

Crystal flakes falling
White blankets sewn with sparkle
Covering the earth

MIRANDA LEIGH

No. 8

Listen to the rain
What is it trying to say
Trying to explain

A LITTLE HAIKU

No. 9

All together torn
Shredded bits and pieces sewn
All together whole

MIRANDA LEIGH

No. 10

From my soul to yours
A collection of my words
Born into fragments

No. 11

A forgotten scent
Inhale the salty fragrance
Exhale ocean air

MIRANDA LEIGH

No. 12

A forgotten sound
Waves crashing upon the shore
Shifting grains of sand

No. 13

I know you prefer
The quiet hum of silence
Your thoughts the lyrics

MIRANDA LEIGH

No. 14

Our lives put on pause
Fingers anxious to press play
Ready to resume

No. 15

Vivid colors fade
In a melancholy mood
All that's left is grey

MIRANDA LEIGH

No. 16

Hidden stars above
Waiting for the chance to shine
Magic in the sky

A LITTLE HAIKU

No. 17

Sun setting in waves
Of splendid colors scattered
Infinite canvas

MIRANDA LEIGH

No. 18

Trees grow bare as bones
When winter breathes, they shiver
We grow cold as stone

A LITTLE HAIKU

No. 19

Do they resonate
Do they reach inside your skin
Settle in your soul

MIRANDA LEIGH

No. 20

Rise and fall of breath
As it fills, as it empties
Keeping you alive

No. 21

Heart full of desire
Blood pumping through veins of fire
Burning and bleeding

MIRANDA LEIGH

No. 22

A break in the sky
Tear drops fall from clouds above
Sorrow feeds the seeds

A LITTLE HAIKU

No. 23

We fit perfectly
Three souls in sink, harmony
A puzzle complete

No. 24

I invest in you
Give all that I am to you
Smile when you prosper

No. 25

Together let's make
Love spread, give wings to wildfire
Give light to dark

MIRANDA LEIGH

No. 26

How many loved ones
Will be taken, will be lost
So many loved ones

No. 27

Through the misty fog
In the haze of dusk to dawn
Just beyond my reach

No. 28

I lost my footing
When I stumbled into you
I began to fall

No. 29

A life without you
Difficult to live, to breathe
Lungs gasping for air

No. 30

I'm an open book
Read me cover to cover
Written just for you

No. 31

Life in a painting
With each stroke the colors dance
Create a vision

MIRANDA LEIGH

No. 32

Looming clouds of fear
Thunderous paranoia
Longing for clear skies

No. 33

I can hear your heart
Speak, a gentle loving tone
Words a steady beat

MIRANDA LEIGH

No. 34

I can't wait to wake
Open my eyes to your love
Spend each day with you

No. 35

A time for giving
A day, a season to be
Ever so grateful

MIRANDA LEIGH

No. 36

Oh the Universe
A bright soul full of magic
Stars the shining pulse

No. 37

The gates are open
For the words to walk through
Free to find their way

MIRANDA LEIGH

No. 38

Restless state of mind
Words stirring, trying to find
Their way to stillness

No. 39

An apology
From my beating heart to yours
Let's make love not war

No. 40

Just a little broken
Bruised and tender, fractured heart
Not beyond repair

A LITTLE HAIKU

No. 41

I can't sleep without
You lying next to me, eyes closed
Breath and dreams aligned

MIRANDA LEIGH

No. 42

Constellations made
Walking stardust skin and bones
Souls in shapes of stars

A LITTLE HAIKU

No. 43

Feel the beat of soul
Energy from head to toe
Life of the lyrics

MIRANDA LEIGH

No. 44

Seeking the unknown
In you, I found all that I
Needed, I found home

No. 45

Just counting the stars
One to a million casting
Wishes and shadows

MIRANDA LEIGH

No. 46

Longing to be seen
Only shadows and whispers
Longing to be heard

A LITTLE HAIKU

No. 47

If I stay longer
Dive deeper, will I become
The tide, taste of sea

MIRANDA LEIGH

No. 48

Ocean holds the key
Lost and churning with the tides
Buried in the sand

No. 49

Your gaze upon me
Candle light casting shadows
Flame that never dims

MIRANDA LEIGH

No. 50

How I love to plant
Surprises, watch your eyes light
Smile, as your smile grows

A LITTLE HAIKU

No. 51

Stillness unravels
I can feel the pause of life
Yet, I feel alive

No. 52

Ever so grateful

Each breath, a gift, I exhale

Love from a distance

No. 53

An unspoken rhyme
Stillness wrapped in gratitude
Steady breath of time

MIRANDA LEIGH

No. 54

Cried too many days
Blood stained grief, tear stained pillow
Rivers of sorrow

No. 55

Time in a bottle
Never to be forgotten
Tossed into the sea

MIRANDA LEIGH

No. 56

Stuck in Haiku mode
Can't stop counting syllables
No desire to stop

No. 57

Alone, not lonely
As long as I have your love
In my possession

MIRANDA LEIGH

No. 58

Need a shooting star
Need a magic wand to wave
Have a wish to make

No. 59

Please don't be gone long
Seconds, minutes, but not hours
Your absence profound

MIRANDA LEIGH

No. 60

Rattled to the core
Scared and shaken, rise above
Stronger than before

No. 61

Wandering the streets
Wondering when we would meet
Waiting for this day

MIRANDA LEIGH

No. 62

Run, run like the wind
Don't get stuck in the quicksand
Barefoot and breathless

A LITTLE HAIKU

No. 63

I see only eyes
Your eyes looking back at me
Reflection of love

MIRANDA LEIGH

No. 64

Stripped down to the bones
Courage, love, kindness, power
What's in the marrow

No. 65

Believe in loving
Whole hearted giving, living
Life beyond measure

MIRANDA LEIGH

No. 66

Your tears from my eyes
Two aching throbbing hearts, one
Your blood is my blood

A LITTLE HAIKU

No. 67

One million pieces
Shattered heart on your behalf
Your pain is my pain

No. 68

End of tunnel, light
Don't be afraid of the dark
Focus on the light

No. 69

Falling down, the sky
Little golden pieces, stars
Sink into the earth

MIRANDA LEIGH

No. 70

Experiences
The ones that almost break you
Make you grow stronger

No. 71

Learn to simplify
Silence the voice of busy
Less is often more

MIRANDA LEIGH

No. 72

Twelve years have flown by
Love has grown beyond measure
Filled me to the brim

No. 73

Many call them weeds
I call them wishes to be
Granted by the breeze

No. 74

Days have disappeared
Vanished, gone without a trace
Ghosts of yesterday

No. 75

I see your eyes roam
Thirsty and searching, for more
Absorbing it all

No. 76

Stronger than you think
Iron will, quiet power
Force driven by love

No. 77

Together we bleed
Melt into one another
Two hearts beat as one

No. 78

As the sun rises
Colors scatter through the trees
Open your eyes, see

A LITTLE HAIKU

No. 79

Somewhere in between
My skin ends and yours begins
Lost in each other

MIRANDA LEIGH

No. 80

Unspoken promise
I'll be here always, waiting
When you come to me

No. 81

Come, escape the cold
Bones chilled by frozen marrow
Let me keep you warm

MIRANDA LEIGH

No. 82

Want to celebrate
Life and love, laugh, be merry
To see your faces

No. 83

My heart beats for you
No matter the miles between
Love goes the distance

MIRANDA LEIGH

No. 84

Feet on solid ground
Swift, cold water current tried
To pull me under

No. 85

Will never forget
The feel of your hand in mine
The touch of your love

No. 86

Eyes closed blink open
Time to see, hear, feel, write, be
Who you've always been

No. 87

I am different
I don't see what you see
Quite the opposite

MIRANDA LEIGH

No. 88

Little bothered by
Idea of following
Not sure I follow

No. 89

A solar being
Powered by the sun, recharged
Ready to shine bright

MIRANDA LEIGH

No. 90

Out of the shadows
I walk, I run, I fly free
Broken wings spread wide

No. 91

I'll be your constant
Definition of always
That's me beside you

MIRANDA LEIGH

No. 92

Slow and steady burn
Embers to dancing flame, fire
Heat to keep you warm

No. 93

Words just a river
Meandering through my brain
Can't fight the current

No. 94

Like the ocean tide
Restless, wild, peaceful and calm
I exist in waves

No. 95

I'll search forever
To the edge of time and past
Seek until I find

MIRANDA LEIGH

No. 96

Extinguish my flame
Turn me to smoke and ash, try
I will reignite

No. 97

Dancing on rooftops
Smiles on faces, clouds in hair
Sunset lights the way

MIRANDA LEIGH

No. 98

Nothing left to say
I worry about this day
When it's all been said

No. 99

Want to smell the air
Inhale the scent of season
Feel it touch my face

No. 100

Can we sleep like this
Unaware of time passing
You wrapped around me

No. 101

Hand upon my heart
I swear with all that I am
You are all I need

No. 102

No longer have bones
To frame my soul, no body
To carry my load

No. 103

The tallest tree alone
No forest for protection
Only earth and sky

MIRANDA LEIGH

No. 104

Ocean is alive
Steady rhythmic breath in waves
Shallow to the deep

No. 105

I'm counting again
Always counting syllables
Words lined with numbers

MIRANDA LEIGH

No. 106

Close your eyes, inhale
Stop the racing words, exhale
Let sleep have its way

No. 107

Sun salutation
With an inhale rise above
Reach for the sun, sky

MIRANDA LEIGH

No. 108

Roots deeply buried
Grasping for earth, crumbled dirt
Building foundation

No. 109

Eyes a smoky haze
Full of lust or maybe love
Lips on burning skin

MIRANDA LEIGH

No. 110

There you sit across
The checkerboard deep in thought
Found my mate for life

No. 111

When I heard your heart
Beating inside of me, my
Own heart paused in awe

MIRANDA LEIGH

No. 112

I can see through you
As if you're a crystal ball
I see my future

No. 113

Wild winds are blowing
Recklessly waving branches
Giving directions

MIRANDA LEIGH

No. 114

You loved me even
Then, when I was just a mess
To clean up after

No. 115

If only I had
A pot of golden stars, luck
And wishes to give

MIRANDA LEIGH

No. 116

How rarely I step
Outside to see the beauty
The magic of night

No. 117

Listen to me now
Never feel guilt for having
A voice, speak your mind

MIRANDA LEIGH

No. 118

Hands reach, fingers trace
Silhouettes in the darkness
Shadows in the sheets

No. 119

Time a precious gift
Not to be wasted, cherish
Every moment

MIRANDA LEIGH

No. 120

When the world feels safe
I will run wild into it
Wanderlust set free

No. 121

Tried putting myself
In your shoes, they didn't fit
I just can't imagine

No. 122

In the thick of it
The weeds before the forest
Almost in the clear

No. 123

Dripping, melting ice
From the branches to the earth
Trees cold and weeping

MIRANDA LEIGH

No. 124

Ideas dead, gone
Graveyard in your mind, buried
Ghosts of afterthoughts

No. 125

We all start somewhere
Little seeds planted with hope
For infinite growth

No. 126

Your face held the smile
The one to light up my world
To erase my frown

No. 127

Write about nothing
Even nothing is something
Worth writing about

MIRANDA LEIGH

No. 128

I see you as brave
You speak all the hidden truths
You give wings to words

No. 129

Heart an open wound
Bleeding and pumping only
Love to stay alive

MIRANDA LEIGH

No. 130

May these words be like
Seeds, as you read you water
Feel them grow inside

No. 131

Focused on the words
I missed the quiet rhythm
I missed the feeling

MIRANDA LEIGH

No. 132

Allow it to be
Don't force it to be, open
Yourself to the flow

No. 133

Kindness of strangers
Something to be grateful for
Hearts of the unknown

MIRANDA LEIGH

No. 134

I will burn brighter
In the face of fear, of doubt
I will grow brighter

No. 135

Outside looking in
No light streaming from windows
There's nobody home

MIRANDA LEIGH

No. 136

How deep is the snow
Can you feel the earth below
Numb toes tread lightly

No. 137

Stop the train of thought
In its tracks, no good will come
From that direction

MIRANDA LEIGH

No. 138

Promise I will try
With all my heart, all my soul
Not to break again

No. 139

We flow like rivers
Find our way around and through
Forest to the sea

MIRANDA LEIGH

No. 140

Hate is a disease
A sickness we must not spread
Love, an antidote

No. 141

The voice of time speaks
In numbers that add up to
Life in memories

MIRANDA LEIGH

No. 142

Count the seconds, count
The faces, count the voices
Photos of places

No. 143

Okay to differ
Find some common ground, unite
Light of compromise

MIRANDA LEIGH

No. 144

Let's give love to hate
Watch as hate disintegrates
A puddle of peace

No. 145

Gratitude for guilt
A substitution needed
A switch of the mind

MIRANDA LEIGH

No. 146

A new beginning
A time to tear down old walls
A time to rebuild

No. 147

When will it be time
To let your dreams lead the way
New reality

MIRANDA LEIGH

No. 148

I hear all the words
At once, a jumble of thoughts
Fighting for freedom

A LITTLE HAIKU

No. 149

I will stay for love
I will give everything
And know its value

MIRANDA LEIGH

No. 150

I'll be the light you
Seek, the golden rays to shine
Upon your darkness

No. 151

I will run with you
Or go slowly if you choose
To the end and back

MIRANDA LEIGH

No. 152

If you must wake me
Please do so with desire
Sleeping skin awaits

No. 153

The quiet places
Find them, listen to the voice
Inside the silence

MIRANDA LEIGH

No. 154

Fill all the pages
A voice planted on paper
Seeds and syllables

No. 155

At a loss for words
A sponge soaking in feelings
Overcome with love

MIRANDA LEIGH

No. 156

How we fascinate
Art composed of energy
Mystery beings

No. 157

It is mine alone
A practice created by
My mind, body, soul

No. 158

I can see you've changed
Your energy has shifted
In all the right ways

No. 159

Light dances on lids
Of closed eyes, lashes begin
To flutter, awake

MIRANDA LEIGH

No. 160

End of winter, wait
Days, nights, minutes, hours freeze
One day melt as one

No. 161

Maybe what felt like
Anger was just loneliness
Maybe you were missed

MIRANDA LEIGH

No. 162

Give the gift of love

Wrapped as you see fit, always

A need and a want

No. 163

So much could be said
All the words for gratitude
Running through my head

MIRANDA LEIGH

No. 164

Drowning in quiet
Ears alert for any noise
A reason to breathe

No. 165

Feelings navigate

From the empty to the full

Find a way to pour

MIRANDA LEIGH

No. 166

Shifting, drifting grains
Of energy, sands sifting
Through fingers of time

No. 167

Eyes seem to be stuck
Wide with wonder, glued upon
The light before me

MIRANDA LEIGH

No. 168

Full of muses, life
Find them, follow them, let them
Inspire your art

No. 169

Chemicals react
Evoke our senses, with just
The right formula

MIRANDA LEIGH

No. 170

Skin traced by fingertips
Limbs and sheets, tangled shadows
Hidden hearts collide

No. 171

Twenty five years, friends
If I could go back, repeat
With you by my side

No. 172

You are an artist
Always embrace that, create
As only you can

No. 173

Hours left to live
Only hours to love you
I will hold on tight

MIRANDA LEIGH

No. 174

Only hours left
Turn the music up, full blast
Soundtrack of your life

No. 175

Swimming in the sea
Waiting to begin again
Bathing in beauty

MIRANDA LEIGH

No. 176

Physical beings
Bodies, skin and bones, merely
Vessels for much more

No. 177

If I had to choose
My last words would be to you
This is not goodbye

MIRANDA LEIGH

No. 178

We are magnetic
Pools of energy, forces
Breathing and pulling

No. 179

He could fill the room
With his love, with his laughter
He would give the moon

MIRANDA LEIGH

No. 180

Mass of energy
Along for the ride, pulled by
Gravity of time

No. 181

One day by the sea
Waves crashing, sun shimmering
There, you will find me

MIRANDA LEIGH

No. 182

Days melt into nights
Sun rises from the shadows
Again and again

No. 183

Illumination
Glowing, gleaming light of love
Fire beneath skin

MIRANDA LEIGH

No. 184

Our world as it spins
Planet, country, state, city
Just geography

No. 185

All smoke, no substance
Reaching, grasping hands, empty
Chasing hollow dreams

MIRANDA LEIGH

No. 186

First inhale of spring
Fills desperate, longing lungs
With air and promise

No. 187

If I could travel
To another place and time
Who would I become

No. 188

Stars beware of stones
Flying through the air, full speed
Without direction

No. 189

Trace the lines of life
Branches down to roots, to seeds
Origin of skin

MIRANDA LEIGH

No. 190

Old faded photos
Ripped up jeans and memories
Untold stories found

No. 191

Gaze lands upon you
Across the room, a flicker
Of recognition

MIRANDA LEIGH

No. 192

Sun of summer, come
Come now, blaze through time and space
Warm my skin and bones

A LITTLE HAIKU

No. 193

Generosity
A planet fueled by giving
Art of survival

MIRANDA LEIGH

No. 194

Bathe in contentment
What creates this calming sea
Waves of you and me

No. 195

Heart broken, soul sick
Drowning in a sea of loss
Grief a storm of ache

MIRANDA LEIGH

No. 196

Time can fade or grow
Feelings, seeds of love and hate
Dying or blooming

No. 197

A broken record
Words stuck on repeat, failing
To mean anything

MIRANDA LEIGH

No. 198

People of the world
Embrace your differences
Let them give you strength

No. 199

People of the world
Build each other up, higher
Spread smiles, love and laughter

No. 200

People of the world
We have potential to grow
To achieve great things

No. 201

Believe in yourself
Free your insecurities
Feel your soul, alive

MIRANDA LEIGH

No. 202

Reasons I love you
I could go on forever
The list, infinite

No. 203

Do we remember
Sleep, dreams, false realities
Eyes closed, mind streaming

No. 204

Flashbacks of the breaks
The many times I shattered
Made whole by your love

No. 205

Why does time erase
The good, but not the bad, heal
Only shallow wounds

MIRANDA LEIGH

No. 206

Clouds be curtains, grey
Parted just enough, not wide
Star to shine on stage

No. 207

Looking for shadows
But they don't seem to follow
Lost them in the light

MIRANDA LEIGH

No. 208

Truth never spoken
Words never written in stone
Still somehow, you know

No. 209

Universe in waves
Softly speaking in whispers
Sounds your soul can feel

MIRANDA LEIGH

No. 210

Traveling feet, soles
Wearing thin along the road
Smile growing by miles

No. 211

Hidden colors shine
Brought to life by light of day
Blinded by rainbows

MIRANDA LEIGH

No. 212

Wrap your brain around
All that it's capable of
Embrace the unknown

No. 213

Where should I begin
Place my loving hands to heal
Which scar speaks loudest

MIRANDA LEIGH

No. 214

Dust accumulates
Layered within, bones like shelves
In need of cleaning

No. 215

Feel all colors swirl
A painting inside expressed
Drawn to black and white

MIRANDA LEIGH

No. 216

Then it all came back
Full speed, life in a hurry
Time no longer still

No. 217

Be the soaking sponge
Absorb infinite knowledge
I will learn from you

MIRANDA LEIGH

No. 218

Manifest your dreams
Plant the seeds and watch them grow
Big and beautiful

No. 219

Toes in foreign sand
Waves spoken in foreign tongue
Sails wandering sea

No. 220

Floating through this life
Guided by intuition
Feathers on a whim

No. 221

Mother and daughter
Give and take, love becomes strength
Bond unbreakable

MIRANDA LEIGH

No. 222

Sparks thrown by lust, burst
Into flames of love, burning
Melting soul to soul

No. 223

Day, week, month, a year
She became one with the air
Lungs filled with sorrow

MIRANDA LEIGH

No. 224

Air of turbulence
Fly high above the clouds, look
For silver linings

No. 225

Creatures of habit
Routines and repetitions
Peace in what we know

MIRANDA LEIGH

No. 226

Lifting and sinking
Expanding and contracting
Growing and shrinking

No. 227

Summer day Jeep drive
You, and me in a sundress
Warm breezes and love

MIRANDA LEIGH

No. 228

Gratitude rises
Lifts you, fills you, shines and spreads
Sunlight to surface

ABOUT THE AUTHOR

I am the author of A Soul Adrift, A Soul Defined, A Soul Immersed, and A Little Haiku, a massage therapist and yoga instructor. I have been writing poetry since I was 17. My passions include poetry, yoga, family, music, sunshine, the ocean, and life in general. I have a loving husband and daughter that inspire me every day. I am an optimist who believes in the power of positivity.

Made in the USA
Monee, IL
12 September 2021